# Handyman Pricing Handbook

Be confident about your pricing
and start making money!

# Allen Lee

Handyman Pricing Handbook

I dedicate this book to my mom, Becky Wymore. My mom taught me a lot in life, but one thing she taught me that has had the greatest impact on me is to never give up. Life is full of unexpected setbacks, shortcomings, and failures, but through it all, my mom taught me that if I never give up, I will find success! Life is much like pricing handyman jobs. You will undoubtedly fail at times, you will price jobs way too low, and you will scare away some clients, but all in all, if you never give up and find what works for you, you will find success. Thanks, Mom! Love ya!

# Contents

# Foreword

Several years ago, I found Allen Lee on YouTube. Having really enjoyed his down-to-earth style and Christian approach to contracting, I joined his group on Facebook and have enjoyed moderating there for quite some time now. Allen's educational videos and writings have been very helpful to me in my business, as sometimes we get stuck in our own ways or quite possibly just haven't learned there can be a better way to do something! Gaining another's perspective can be so valuable. Even if you've been doing this trade your entire life, someone can suddenly show you another way that you've never thought of before and save you time, money, and frustration.

Allen's group, The Handyman Journey, on Facebook has become a huge resource for contractors and handymen as a place where one can post questions and actually receive help and not ridicule, and as such, it has become my favorite over the last years.

I've been a general contractor in Oklahoma for around a decade now, and it has been one of the most enjoyable and rewarding jobs I have ever had. Being your own boss has its own frustrations and tough times, but the payoff is so great! Freedom from a nine-to-five, even when it may mean you choose an occasional twelve-to-fourteen-hour day somehow just feels so fantastic. The ability to repair many things that others may not have the skill to do adds a lot to the feeling of accomplishment that this profession provides.

Pricing our jobs is a continual learning process. I've adjusted and modified my methods over and over through the years.

Allen has written this fantastic book to give an outline to help you determine the method that will work the best for you as well as give you the confidence to quote at the rate your business needs to thrive! He shares many of his experiences as well as others' methods in this book, to help you find the perfect strategy to simplify your estimating and the invoicing process and save you as much time as possible. This book will be a tremendous resource to starting and growing your handyman business.

Happy contracting!

Josef Millis,
Millis Construction

# Introduction

Have you ever said to yourself, "I have no clue what to charge as a handyman" or "I feel bad charging what I need to charge" or even "I feel like I am undercharging, but I have no clue, and I don't feel like people will pay me for what I need to make"? If you are reading this book, I bet you have thought these thoughts a time or two. I know this because I have thought those exact same things in my own handyman business more times than a few!

I have personally talked to and consulted thousands of different people on their handyman businesses, and one of the biggest questions I hear from them revolves around pricing handyman jobs and not feeling confident in charging what they need to charge or flat-out not knowing what they should charge.

I don't know if you caught the common denominator in those three things that I often hear from handyman business owners, but it is the words, "I feel." The biggest problem for most handyman business owners—all business owners, for that matter—is they rely on their feelings rather than what they know for certain.

A lot of our fears, the things that hold us back, are defeated by knowledge; that is what this book is all about, turning your feelings into proper knowledge. Knowledge that will empower you, free you, and allow you and your business to grow to heights that you never imagined, and it all starts with pricing. So, let's get to pricing correctly, so we can start serving others more efficiently.

Before we get into the "*how*" of setting our pricing, let's cover a few mindset issues that are at the core of pricing correctly.

# Establishing Your Pricing—The Basics

The basis of having confidence in your pricing for your handyman business is the knowledge that you are charging what you need to charge and what is fair. The question is how do you gain that knowledge? We are going to answer that very question in this book.

Everyone has gut feelings, and those are great. They help us make quick decisions and help guide us down certain paths in life, but sometimes you need more than just a gut feeling. It starts with a gut feeling, but you also need knowledge.

What do gut feelings and knowledge have to do with pricing handyman jobs? Everything. When most people start a handyman business, they pull a number from thin air and think to themselves, "*I will charge x amount of dollars because that is way more than I used to make. I'll be rolling in the dough.*"

This was exactly my thought when I first started up my business too. I quickly came to realize that this thought failed me fairly quickly when I saw that there was more money coming out of the business than was going in. I was actually losing money. Why would I want to go into business for myself to lose money?

This is when I dug deep into learning about this pricing topic, and I realized that pricing had as much to do with mindset as it did with the actual number I charged. We are going to start on mindset and then move into figuring out our numbers.

# Pricing Mindset

The first thing you need to hear and understand is that *you* are valuable, what you do is valuable, and what you know is valuable. It is up to you to express that value to the client. Most people struggle to believe that they are valuable in what they do and offer, and that is the first thing you need to change your mind about.

When people call you for service on their home or commercial property, they are calling you because you have something that they do not. Either they don't have the skills to perform the work they need done, or they don't have the time to do it. In any case, you have what they need, and that makes you valuable to them. This is called *perceived value*, and people are willing to pay for the value they perceive in you, so this is the first pricing mindset you need. People are longing to pay you for what you know and do.

The second mindset you need around pricing your handyman business is the knowledge of yourself. You need to know and stand behind what you are offering. Are you offering a fly-by-night handyman, quick, easy, and cheap fix? Or are you offering a "call me, I'm your neighborhood handyman, and I'll do it right" type of work?

A lot of this has to do with falling back on your business's core values. Core values are crucial for a business, because it shows so much of who you are, and it helps your business make decisions. So, if you do not have core values, I recommend creating them—now.

For instance, our slogan for our handyman business is "Your Neighborhood Handyman." Simple and to the point, but it comes from our list of core values and shows not only who we are but what we strive to be and helps establish our value.

Some of our core values are:

- Honor
- Integrity
- Timeliness
- Cleanliness
- Professionalism
- High quality
- Reasonably priced (Underpromise and overdeliver)
- Gets it done no matter what
- Admits when he doesn't know something
- Compassionate
- Has a bigger picture than just being a handyman

To sum up, what our core values help do is help keep our business pointed in the right direction and also help establish our value to our clients.

The first thing you need to do in the subject of gaining knowledge about yourself and your business is establish core values for yourself and your business. This will help you as you grow, especially in establishing your pricing, and very much so in setting up your marketing funnel, which you can learn more about in one of my other books, *Handyman Marketing Handbook*.

This leads us right into learning about our numbers, as that is the next piece of knowledge we need. Get a pen and paper out, or open up a document on your computer, because this is where the fun happens.

# Knowing Your Numbers—Establishing Your Hourly Need

The first thing you need to do in establishing your pricing for your handyman business is to figure out what I call your *hourly need*. You may be thinking, *I heard you're not supposed to charge by the hour.* I would say you're partly right; charging by the job is ultimately better for you and your business, but all pricing needs to start with knowing your hourly need/rate, so that is where we will start. With these formulas, you will be able to know and be confident in what to charge because you have proof to back up your pricing, not just feelings.

Step #1 is writing out all your personal and business expenses. This is best done by printing out your last three months of bank statements, both for yourself and your business. If you haven't started your business, then do this procedure for your personal finances only.

Some of this really depends on the structure of your business. If you are a sole proprietor, you will need to calculate all of your personal expenses, as seen in figure 1. If your business is a corporation, things are pretty much the same, only portrayed in this form in a different way. As a corporation, you will need to pay yourself as an employee of the business, so all your personal expenses will be portrayed as your salary instead of personal expenses.

# Figure 1. Writing out all your expenses

Determine your Hourly Rate as a Handyman
Handyman Journey Pricing
Example

**Personal Expenses:**

| | |
|---|---|
| Mortgage: | 1000 |
| Groceries | 180 |
| Gas | 30 |
| Electric: | 15 |
| Health Insurance | 290 |
| Garbage: | 43 |
| Phone: | 60.4 |
| Giving: | 240 |
| Internet | 65 |
| Water: | 29 |
| Car Insurance: | 120 |
| Life Insurance: | 60 |
| Utility: | 43 |
| Car Gas | 100 |
| Registration: | 12 |
| Eating out: | 50 |
| Savings: | 450 |
| Total: | 2787.4 |

**Business Expenses:**

| | |
|---|---|
| Bus Phone: | 76 |
| Truck Reg | 12 |
| Gen Insurance | 80 |
| Adverting: | 150 |
| Tax: | 750 |
| License Fee: | 14.66 |
| SEP IRA: | 150 |
| Tax prep: | 35 |
| Giving: | 300 |
| Truck Gas: | 240 |
| Total: | 1807.66 |

As a sole proprietor your business expenses and personal expenses are generally the same. *

*Speak to a CPA for exact information on business structure.

You may be asking yourself now, what is the best entity to be as a handyman? That is a question for your CPA. Another huge thing about business is knowing your role and sticking to it, and only it. Far too often, I see people just starting out trying to do it all—their marketing, customer relations, taxes, accounting, etc., all by themselves. The fact of the matter is you cannot do it all yourself.

One exercise that I often coach people on is to think of your business with thirty-plus employees. At that point, would you still have time to do all the tasks your business needs? The answer is *no*, and if you tried to do all those tasks, you would step on so many of your employees' toes that you would have no one who would want to work with you.

This is a big topic that I talked about in my book, *The Handyman Marketing Handbook*, that we just simply cannot do it all, and we shouldn't want to do it all either, because we all have strengths and weaknesses, and the key to success is to operate in our strengths as often as possible and hire people to operate in the things we are weak in.

I know business, and I know how to be a handyman, so that is what I am going to stick to. If you want to be successful, I recommend you stick to what you are strong in as well. This isn't to say that we shouldn't grow in our weaknesses, because we do need to be doing that, but there is a time for everything, and if you want to create something sustainable, get started in your strengths.

Now back to pricing. You may be thinking to yourself, *I don't need to waste my time writing out all my expenses. I'll just focus on making more money than I am spending.* Well, let me tell you, this was my exact train of thought for the first few years of my business, and it led to struggles and more struggles. See, you cannot possibly make more money than you are spending if you don't know how much you are spending to begin with. It's kind of like which came first, the chicken or the egg. It's sort of the same for pricing—you need to know what it will cost to operate in the manner that you need to, so you can know what you need to accurately charge to afford that.

So, make sure you take some time and write out all your expenses. If you haven't yet, put this book down and do it now. This is a very important step that if you choose to skip, you will only be hurting yourself.

The next step in establishing your hourly need, once you have written out all your expenses, is to figure out how many hours you will be working in any given time period. For this example, we will use a month. In any given month, there are, give or take, about 160 working hours (Monday through Friday). As a handyman, you have to know that on average, we will only be about 80 percent efficient, so we will take 80 percent of 160 hours, and we get a total of 128 working hours in a month. The main reason for this 80 percent efficiency is to account for time running to the parts store or time traveling to and from the jobs.

So, let's put these numbers together. For this example, we will say our handyman's name is Jeff, and Jeff calculated his personal expenses at $2,500 a month and his business expenses also at $2,500 a month, so his total expenses would be

$5,000 a month. What Jeff will need to do next is to take his total expense and divide that by the number of working hours in a month. This will give him a base hourly rate. Jeff has now found his hourly need. This will not be what he ends up charging clients; that number will be a little higher, and we will go over how to find that number later in this book.

The calculation looks like this:
$5,000 / 128 = $39.06 / hour (hourly need)


Many other things come into play when you are talking about pricing, like where you are located, demographics, competition, etc., so that's what we will talk about next.

# Establishing Your Pricing—Location

Location is very important when talking about pricing, because many different areas around the world have different restrictions and regulations based on what people can charge for handyman services. For instance, in California, a handyman can only charge $500 per project, while in Florida, there is no limit to what a handyman can charge per project. These laws and regulations vary from state to state and country to country. You will want to make sure you do your own in-depth research, so you know how much you can charge in your area for handyman work. One of the easiest ways to find out what your state's laws are regarding handyman pricing is to search out and talk with your state's contractors board; they will be able to give you the details you are looking for. Another great resource is to contact other handymen in your area and ask them what the laws are regarding a handyman business in your area. Some states that have restrictions on how much you can charge per project also include materials in that calculation of what you can charge, so you will need to take this into account when figuring your hourly rate.

Let's continue our example of handyman Jeff from earlier. We know that handyman Jeff has a base hourly need of $39.06 an hour; let's round this up to $40 an hour. Let's say handyman Jeff lives in California, where the regulations are that he can only charge $500 per project, including labor and materials. So, with that, we can figure that if handyman Jeff charges $40 an hour, the longest a project can take Jeff while staying under the $500 per project limit is 12.5 hours, labor without materials (500 / 40 = 12.5). Now, we obviously are going to up handyman Jeff's hourly rate, but this is an example of his hourly need being put to play.

Knowing your regulations is very important and helps you make better pricing decisions as we set that price more solidly throughout the rest of this book.

# Establishing Your Pricing—Demographics

As a business owner, you have to know your demographics. In a nutshell, demographics is statistical data relating to the population and particular groups within it. Basically, what you need to know here is, can the people in your area, your clients, afford your rate? Can they sustain your needs as a business? This is something you need to research, and if you find out that what you need to charge as a handyman is way out of line with what your clients can afford, then you need to either figure out a way to make your rate less (decrease your expenses) or find a new place to do business.

Most of the time, you are part of the demographics in your area. This means that what you need to charge to support yourself in that area is usually what others are willing to pay in that area. This is called balance. If you find that your rate is way too high, you may be trying to live a little too high on the hog for what your area will allow.

# Establishing Your Pricing—Competition

Competition makes the world go around. People competing with others is a good thing; it creates balance in a way that not too much else can. When you don't have competition, you have a monopoly of one business or entity that has the power to charge insane rates and rake people over the coals.

So, one huge thing to factor in when you are establishing your pricing is competition. You need to know how much competition you have, who they are, what they charge, and what they offer to their clients. One quick tip: do things better than your competition in one or more of those categories, and you will be unusually successful.

Darren Hardy says in his book *The Compound Effect* that what you lack in knowledge or skill, make up for in practice. It doesn't matter what your competition does better than you; you can always beat them by practicing your butt off and focusing on growth where you need it to stand out.

The easy way to find out about your competition is to ask. Simply call them up and ask them questions about their business, although you need to be prepared that some if not most handymen you call will be reluctant to answer your questions. But this means they are scared of competition, and you probably have a leg up on them already.

If you find out that most of your competition is charging $60 an hour, and you can charge less, then that is a leg up. If you need to charge more than your competition, that just means you need to step up your game in some of the things you offer to your clients to make your price worth it to the clients. Always ask yourself, "Why would someone want to hire me?" If you ask yourself that question and come up with a heck of a good answer, you're going to be a huge success.

# Establishing Your Pricing—Breakeven & Profit

Okay, let's get to the meat and potatoes. Once we have figured out our hourly need (total expenses / hours = hourly need), figured out our local laws and regulations, searched out our demographics, and sized up our competition, we are ready to talk about turning that hourly need into an hourly rate.

A simple formula that I teach all my handyman business consultant clients is to take your hourly need and add 20 percent for what I call a "breakeven" number, and 20 percent for profit.

So, let's take handyman Jeff's hourly need of $39.06. If we added 20 percent for breakeven, that would give us $46.87 (39.06 x 1.2 = 46.87) and then add 20 percent to that for profit, we get $56.24 (46.87 x 1.2 = 56.24). Now we are at a price we will be charging the client for our services.

**There are three main numbers you need to know:**

**Hourly need:** This is your base need that you need to charge per hour just to cover expenses. If you were to charge this rate to a client, you may even end up losing money because of incidental and unforeseen costs. In handyman Jeff's case, this number is $39.06.

**Breakeven number:** This is your base hourly need plus 20 percent. The reason why this number is important is that it adds 20 percent to your hourly need to cover those unforeseen costs or incidentals that come up in most jobs. This would be the lowest rate you would want to charge a client for handyman work because with this number, you will most likely just break even, meaning you will just cover your own costs for your labor. Charging this rate would be considered charging cost for a job. In handyman Jeff's case, this number is $46.87.

**Hourly rate:** This is your breakeven number with added 20 percent profit. This number is what I recommend charging your clients for labor. Charging this number will give you the biggest chance at success in your handyman business. When you charge for jobs, you have to factor in profit. Profit is what allows businesses to grow and be fruitful and beneficial to their community. In handyman Jeff's case, this number is $56.24. See figure 2.

# Figure 2. Adding Breakeven and Profit

| Step #1 | Total Expenses | | | | X | Hrs / Month | = | $ Hourly need |
|---|---|---|---|---|---|---|---|---|
| Step #2 | Total Expenses | + | | 20% | X | Hrs / Month | = | $ Break even # |
| Step #3 | 20% breakeven | + | | 20% | X | Hrs / Month | = | $ Hourly Rate |

| | 20% | | Avg Hrs/ Month | $ Per Hour. |
|---|---|---|---|---|
| Total | 5000 | 1000 | 128 | $39.06 |
| 20% Break even | 6000 | 1200 | 128 | $46.88 |
| 20% Profit | 7200 | | 128 | $56.25 |

# How to Charge—

# By the Hour

Now that you know your hourly rate, you are ready to get out there and start estimating handyman jobs. Although I do not recommend charging by the hour for handyman jobs, it can be very helpful to charge by the hour for jobs that you are new at or not as familiar with. When first starting out, charging by the hour may be very beneficial because it is a risk-free way to find out how long jobs will take you to complete. For instance, knowing that Handyman Jeff's hourly rate is $56.24 (lets round to $56 an hour), and he bid one of his first jobs by the job rather than by the hour. Say he bid the job at $100, and it ended up taking him three hours to complete the job. He actually only made $33.30 an hour on that $100 job. But if he was to bid that job by the hour, and it still took him three hours to do, he would have made $168 on that job, which is $56 an hour. The one main reason that I do not recommend people charge by the hour is that as their skill levels increase and they start to be able to complete jobs quicker, they really get a pay decrease, and that's not necessarily fair to the handyman. After all, as we get more skilled, we should be rewarded for that.

So, for instance, let's say handyman Jeff does that same job that used to take him three hours to complete but can now complete it in two hours because he has increased his skills and efficiency. If he were still to charge hourly, he would finish the job in two hours and only charge them $112 for the job, making less money on the same job than he used to make. On the positive side, he now has an extra hour to get to his next job. There is really an argument for both charging hourly and not. So, let's move into charging by the job and see how that can drastically change things.

# How to Charge—

# By the Job

Charging by the job, by far, has the most growth potential when compared to charging by the hour. If you take that same job from our previous example, handyman Jeff can now complete the job that used to take him three hours in two hours, but he charges the same labor rate for the job as he did before. Jeff charges $168 for the job and completes it in two hours, making him $84 an hour, rather than his original $56 hourly rate. Handyman Jeff is now getting paid for his improved skill level and efficiency and has major potential for growth.

Charging by the job gives the handyman many benefits other than just making more per hour, but it also allows the handyman to work in discounts for specific clients if needed or desired and allows the handyman to retain more earnings and give more back to the community.

Charging by the job is best done when you go to look at a job and then figure how many hours it will take you to complete that job. You can then figure out a rate for the job that way. You will also need to factor in the going rate for certain jobs. One great way to look up jobs and prices for those jobs is a website called www.homewyse.com. Homewyse is helpful when figuring a ballpark price for certain jobs in your area; then you can add or subtract from that price as you see fit.

For instance, some jobs may require special skills or techniques that may have a higher going rate in your area. Some of these items may include ceiling fan replacements, toilet replacements, and things like that. These items you may be able to get quick at and make a good figure on because the going rate is much higher than your hourly rate.

# How to Charge—

# Half-Day/Full-Day Rate

Another way some handymen choose to charge is by either a half-day or full-day rate. This is a very simple way of charging and takes a lot of headache out of pricing, but it's not for everyone. Remember, establishing your pricing is really about finding what strategy works best for you and your business.

Charging a half-day and whole-day rate really simplifies things, because it really narrows things down to just a few numbers. Simply, to find your half-day rate, you multiply your hourly rate by four hours (half day), and to find your full-day rate, you multiply your hourly rate by eight hours (full day). It's that simple. I first learned about this way of charging from my friend Josef Millis in Oklahoma. Josef is an amazing business owner who has his fingers in a few different businesses, so he really knows his stuff.

As I have never personally charged this way, I reached out to Josef to get a better grasp of how he implements this pricing strategy. He says that the actual half-day and full-day rate is never discussed with a client; he just simply submits them an estimate for one of those numbers. For instance, if he thinks a job will take him one to four hours, he submits an estimate for his half-day rate, and if he thinks the job will take him five to eight hours, then he submits an estimate for his full-day rate. Whether he gets the job done sooner or not, the price stays the same. Like I said, this type of pricing may not be for everyone, but it sure has its perks.

# Additional Charges—Mileage Charge

It takes money to make money. One thing you will never get away from is operations costs. It will always cost something to get things done, and in our case, it costs money to drive to and from jobs. After all, we need to get to the job, we need to haul our tools to the job, so one very important additional cost that you should be adding to every job estimate is a mileage charge.

This is a simple charge based on the miles that the client's home is from your home or office. We have been including this mileage charge in our estimates for over a year now and have never had anyone bat an eye at it. After all, it takes money to get things done, and we need to not be afraid of charging what it takes to get the things done that we are hired to do. On average, a typical mileage charge is somewhere around fifty cents a mile.

# Additional Charges—Miscellaneous Charges

Miscellaneous charges are just that, charges for miscellaneous items. On every job, you use something that wasn't billed for on the estimate, whether that is a razor blade to clean some caulking up or a few rags to clean a mirror or even one squirt of caulking to fill a gap in a baseboard that wasn't on the original estimate.

The point is that there is always some material that we use that is just too small to add to the estimate, but over time if we didn't bill for it, we would be out some major bucks. Quick story: I used to have an independent contractor who worked for me who never had any materials on his invoices. When I asked him about it, he would always tell me, "Well, I only used a couple of screws," or "I only used a little caulking."

While it might seem insignificant, a few screws at every job turns into a full box pretty soon, and so does a little caulking here or there. The point is that you need to make sure you are charging for what you are using, and the miscellaneous charge on every estimate helps with that. A typical miscellaneous charge is around $10 per $500 estimate, or 2 percent of the estimate total.

# Additional Charges—Debris Haul-Off and Disposal

One thing about handyman work is there is almost always something that needs to be hauled to the trash. Sometimes clients are okay with you dumping trash in their garbage can, but I would not assume that everyone is. Some clients might assume you will be taking away all the garbage, so that is why it is so important to have clear communication on this during the estimate process.

Let's say you are replacing a ceiling fan for the client. You should ask them, "Would you like us to haul that away for you as well?" If they say yes, then you will need to add a debris haul-off and disposal fee to the estimate. If they say no, then they will take care of disposal. I do not recommend adding a haul-off and disposal fee to every estimate, only the jobs that require you to haul things off. But it is good to get in the habit of asking clients when you perform the initial estimate if they have anything that will need to be disposed of when you come and perform the work. That way, there are no surprises for you or the client.

Sometimes I will forget to ask the client this, and when we come and do the work, it is up to me whether I want to bring it up to them or not. For instance, if it is just a small light fixture and I didn't get a disposal fee for it, I will just chalk it up as a learning experience and eat that disposal cost. After all, the item is really small and won't add up to much anyway. On the other hand, if we go and

Handyman Pricing Handbook

replace a prehung door and we do not get a disposal fee, I will bring it up to the client because it is such a huge item.

The way I do that is simply by saying to the client, "I apologize, but I see we did not discuss disposing of this item when we did the original estimate. Would you like me to get rid of it for you, or did you want to do it? If so, the cost for disposal will be $X."

Disposal fees vary greatly from area to area, but the way I calculate it is to figure out how much it will take to dump a full truckload at the dump and factor in how much said debris will take up of a truckload and charge at least that plus a fee for labor for the technician to actually take that truck to the dump and unload it. For instance, if it is one prehung door, I may charge about $55 in a debris haul-off and disposal fee; for a ceiling fan, I may charge $20, and for a lot of fence materials, I will charge upwards of $155, depending on how much there is.

Disposal is another huge thing that most forget to charge for, but it is very important because it is something that costs money to do. There is no hard and fast percentage rule of what to charge for haul-off; you will just have to use your best judgment. This is something that will actually add value to your business because you can phrase it as "We just want to leave this job site cleaner than when we found it."

# Estimating Jobs—

# Stop and Think through

# the Job

One huge thing that you need to do on every job
before you send the estimate, especially when you
are first starting out, is to just stop and think through
the job fully. For me, it helps to go through the job in
my head, as if I am performing the work, from start
to finish. Do you have to roll out a drop cloth? Do
you have to tape anything off? Are there any parts

of the job that might require a special tool or require added time? What will it take to clean up after yourself on the job? Will there be debris that needs to be hauled off?

By doing this thought exercise, you will most likely catch some things that you originally overlooked when first creating this estimate. This will ultimately make you more money and save you money.

# Estimating Jobs—Minimum Charge

The question comes up a lot, "Should I have a minimum charge for handyman jobs?" The simple answer is yes. The long answer is, at the end of the day, some clients will call you for super-small jobs, like needing one picture hung on the wall. While we are in business to help all people with all types of handyman jobs, we need to make sure the jobs we go and do are mutually beneficial, meaning they are good for the client and for us. This keeps everyone happy.

Say a client calls you, and they only want one picture hung. The main question would then be what do you charge. In handyman Jeff's example, is he to charge his hourly rate of $56? Should he only charge the time he is at the job? So, if he gets the picture hung in ten minutes, is he to charge $9.33 for that job ($56 / 6 = $9.33)? I would say if he charged the client $9.33, the client would think that was too cheap for this work. After all, it's not even a $10 bill.

Should Jeff then charge an hour rate as his minimum? Well, if so, the client might think $56 is a little steep just to hang one picture that only took Jeff ten minutes to complete. So, this is the conundrum. There is, like many things, no hard and fast rule as to how you should charge for small jobs like this or even that you need to charge a minimum at all. At the end of the day, if you are good with charging $9.33 to hang one picture, that is fine. What matters is if it feels good to you in your heart. After that, it doesn't matter what anyone else thinks about it. You do you.

I want to talk for a second about how I do minimum charges and how I portray that to the client. Again, this may not work for you, and that's okay. There is more than one way to skin a cat. Not that I have tried.

When potential clients call me up for small repairs or jobs, I inform them that we have a minimum; for us, it is a minimum that is equivalent to two hours of our labor, but when I tell them the minimum, I do not tell them it is a two-hour minimum. I just give them the price. I proceed to tell them that we have this minimum, so I ask them if they might have any additional things that we can do to fulfill this minimum. After all, I wouldn't want to charge them two hours of labor for just a ten-minute job. Phrasing this this way has been tremendous and even turned a small ten-minute job that they originally called about into a $400 or $500 job.

Most of the time, when people call you, they are calling with their sights laser focused on the job they are calling about and forget the other things their house might need done. Posing questions like this can jog their memories to what else they need done and thus turns into more work for you. This is a topic I cover very in depth in the *Handyman Sales Handbook*, which is the art of upselling.

I have seen minimum charges range all over the board, so there is no right or wrong way to do it. At the end of the day, you just need to make sure you are getting paid for the work you are going out to do. Some handymen charge 20 percent over their hourly rate for the first hour and then their hourly rate for each hour after that. Some charge a flat two-hour minimum, while some just do straight hourly and would charge that $9.33 for a ten-minute job.

Our minimum job price also includes all our added fees like mileage charge and miscellaneous supplies fee, so the total will come out to a few dollars over our two-hour rate.

# Writing Estimates—

# Brief How-To

Writing estimates will not be something I cover too in depth in this book because it is covered very in depth, along with the whole estimate process in the next book of The Handyman Journey series, entitled *Handyman Sales Handbook* (to be released in late-2022).

As important as it is, I wanted to talk about it in this book. I have used many different platforms to write estimates, and I wanted to briefly touch on and share some pros and cons of each and then let you know about the platform I currently use and why.

**Google Docs:** Google Docs is what I used when I first started my handyman to write and deliver estimates. This was a super-simple platform. I created my own template for an estimate and filled in the customer's information and pricing info and then would email it to the client as a PDF. This way of creating estimates was not very sustainable at all, mainly because saving each Google Doc for records took up a lot of space on my computer. But it was free, so that was a great part about it.

**Wave Apps:** Wave Apps is an online platform that, at the time, only provided invoicing and estimating. I believe now it does a whole lot more like accounting. Wave Apps solved one problem that Google Docs didn't have, and that was the saving and auto-sending of all estimates and invoices, so that is why I switched to it. I used it for about a year. It was also free at the time I used it, so that was nice, but I ended up switching to the next estimating software to take advantage of one tool it did not provide.

**Joist:** Joist is an awesome invoicing and estimating software that provides web and mobile phone use, so that is the main reason that I switched to it from Wave Apps. It is so nice to be able to edit or create invoices or estimates while out in the field from your phone. Joist was also free at the time, but I believe they have a paid option now.

**Markate:** In my eyes, Markate is the number-one handyman invoicing and estimating software, but it is not just that; it is a complete CRM, and that is the main reason I ultimately switched to it. Markate is a paid platform, but the benefits from it completely make it worthwhile. A CRM is a customer-relations management tool that stores all of your customers' data for use down the road. This also allows you to do direct marketing to people who are on your clients list, a major tool when it comes to reestablishing cold leads. I am currently working with Markate to make the business-growth side of it much stronger and more robust, so that we as business owners could bring up a few reports and figure out where we need to focus more to grow our business. These business-growth features from *The Handyman Journey* tied with Markate will make it an ultimate and affordable, ultra-necessary handyman business tool.

The Handyman Journey has worked with Markate to get readers of this book a special discount. Signing up through The Handyman Journey guarantees you a free 14-day trial of Markate AND 10% off your first month. Use this affiliate link to get that deal: https://www.markate.com/?aff=AllenLee

# CompanyCam

If you haven't heard of Company Cam or given them a try, you need to give them a try. I've worked with them to get readers of this book a special deal that I will share more about below. CompanyCam is a must have addition to your sales process, in short it is an app that easily organizes all your job and company photos.

Before CompanyCam our photo organization and sharing was all over the map and at times was frustrating! The way we used to do photos of jobs was each person would take photos on his or her phone and they would be the only ones that had access to those photos unless someone else on the team thought to ask them for it, in that case we would text or email it to them. This would unfortunately lead to the technician not having the photos he needs before performing the job, or the estimator would not have the photos he needs when estimating the job.

CompanyCam has changed the way we do business by allowing us to create online files for each client and anyone on our team can add photos or videos to that file and it instantly shares the information with everyone on our team!

CompanyCam is a huge part of our sales process because it makes photo gathering and sharing so simple. A client calls our office and talks with our CSR, our CSR takes their info and asks them for photos, she then creates a file for that client on CompanyCam and then uploads the photos there. When it comes time for our estimator to call that client he can simply open CompanyCam and access all the photos in that clients file as well as any additional notes the CSR wrote in there and add additional photos he may take while at the clients home.

Likewise when the technician is looking through the jobs he will be performing soon he can access that same file in CompanyCam and see the photos and notes that have been added by the other team members. When the technician is out on the job he can take before during and after photos of the project in CompanyCam and can also take pictures of any additional work that the client would like done and all he needs to do is inform the estimator that the client would like additional work done and that there are pictures in CompanyCam with needed notes. As you can see CompanyCam makes the whole process run so much smoother!

Like I said earlier, I have been working with CompanyCam to get readers of this book a special deal on their software. Signing up through The Handyman Journey guarantees you a free 14-day trial of CompanyCam AND 50% off your first two (2) months. Use this affiliate link to get that deal: https://companycam.com/handymanjourney

# The Handyman Journey Pricing Guide

Below is The Handyman Journey Pricing Guide. This list is just a ballpark list and should not be taken as solid figures. We have had many people ask for a simple pricing guide that would give them a ballpark figure on what to charge for certain jobs. Take this list with a grain of salt, though. No one knows your business and what it should be charging better than you. Use the techniques and skills that you learned in this book to narrow down and define your exact pricing, but feel free to use this pricing guide as a starting place.

# Pricing Guide:

## Bathroom:

- Bathroom faucet replacement/installation - **$100**
- Sink drain replacement/installation - **$100–$250**
- Minor sink drain cleaning (nothing major) - **$65**
- Bathroom sink replacement/installation - **$200–$350**
- Bathroom vanity replacement/installation - **$300–$400**
- Towel bar replacement/installation - **$45**
- GFCI outlet replacement/installation - **$120**
- Water supply valve (angle stop valve) replacement - **$85**
- Water-supply hoses replacement/installation - **$35**
- Medicine cabinet replacement/installation - **$100–$200**
- Bathroom mirror replacement/installation - **$75–$175**
- Toilet replacement/installation - **$145**
- Toilet flange (closet flange) replacement/repair - **$185–$300**
- Toilet flush/fill valve replacement - **$90**
- Toilet wax ring replacement - **$100**

- Shower cartridge replacement (shower leaking when valve turned off/valve not turning/shower inoperative) - **$150–$250**
- Shower head replacement - **$45**
- Shower/bathtub recaulking - **$130–$200**
- Shower curtain installation - **$65**
- Shower door replacement/installation - **$150–$300**
- Bathroom exhaust vent fan installation with wiring - **$200–$300**
- Bathroom light fixture replacement/installation - **$85**

# Kitchen:

- Refrigerator water supply valve (angle stop valve) replacement - **$85**
- Cabinet/drawer pull/knob installation - **$6–$10 per pull**
- Cabinet hinge replacement - **$6–10 per hinge set**
- GFCI outlet replacement/installation - **$120**
- Kitchen light fixture replacement/installation - **$85**
- Dishwasher replacement - **$150–$250**
- Dishwasher electrical outlet installation - **$120**
- Faucet replacement/installation - **$145**
- Minor sink drain cleaning (nothing major) - **$65**
- Kitchen sink replacement/installation - **$200–$350**

- Sink drain replacement/installation - **$100–$250**
- Garbage disposal replacement/installation - **$125**
- Water supply valve (angle stop valve) replacement - **$85**
- Water supply hoses replacement/installation - **$35**
- Dishwasher air gap clean or replacement (water spills into sink while dishwasher is draining) - **$100**
- Sink-mounted soap dispenser replacement/installation - **$45–$150**
- Over-the-range microwave replacement/installation - **$155**
- Over-the-range vent hood replacement/installation - **$125**

# Common Rooms:

- Picture/mirror mounting/hanging - **$15 per picture (depends on size)**
- Light fixture replacement/installation - **$85**
- New electrical wires run for lights/TVs/ceiling fans - **$250–$450 depending on access**
- Electrical outlet replacement/installation - **$75 (replace), $180 new wires (not in attic)**
- Light switch replacement/installation - **$75**
- Furniture assembly - **depends on size**

- TV mounting - **$125**
- Ceiling fan replacement/installation - **$150**
- Interior door replacement - **$120**
- Doorknob/deadbolt replacement/installation - **$85**
- Electronic deadbolt installation - **$90**
- Trim/casing/baseboard replacement/installation - **$100–$300, depends on amount**
- Minor drywall repair (up to 6' x 6') (larger may be doable if needed) - **$200–$400, depends on size**
- Blinds/curtains hung/installation - **$75**
- Can lighting installation - **$85 per light**
- Sliding glass door roller replacement (Door hard to roll) - **$100–$200**
- Prehung door replacement - **$350**

# Exterior Work:

- Up to 20' fence replacement - **$200–$300 per 8-foot panel**
- Fence repair (1 to 4 broken fenceposts) (galvanized fencepost install) - **$145 per galvanized fencepost**
- Sprinkler line repair - **$75–$300**
- Sprinkler head replacement - **$85**
- Sprinkler drip replacement/repair - **$75–$180**
- Sprinkler valve replacement - **$135**
- Sprinkler timer replacement/installation - **$125**
- Exterior caulking - **$75–$200**

- Hose spigot replacement - **$75**
- Main water valve repacking (water valve leaking) depending on the type of valve - **$155**
- Gate rebuild - **$200**
- Gate rebuild with post replacement - **$350–$450 depending on complexity**
- Backyard cleanup - depends (don't forget dump fee) - **about $50–$75 per pickup load**

# Questions From Handymen

I thought it would be a great addition to this handbook and a great help to the handyman community to include questions from people who are actively in the field, performing handyman work from all around the world. So, here I will be answering questions and providing my answers to those questions. These questions are taken mainly from our online Facebook Handyman Journey mastermind group, which is, at the time of writing this book, just over five thousand members, handymen from all around the world looking to improve their knowledge and skills.

**Brian Davis from Florida asks:**

*Are there certain jobs that could warrant charging more than my hourly rate? Not that I charge by the hour, but in general, if I was going to charge more than my hourly rate, would you say there are some jobs where that is okay, based on the skill level of the job, level of difficulty, things like that?*

Great question, Brian. You probably already got your answer after reading this book, but my answer is yes, there are many jobs for which you can charge more than your hourly rate, and you pinned it right on the head. Usually those jobs require extra or specialized skills. Usually anything requiring electrical or plumbing work will be able to be billed at a much higher rate than your hourly rate, but this is really accomplished through charging by the job instead of by the hour. For instance, let's take a simple outlet replacement. After you get good at it, it will only take you about fifteen minutes to complete, if everything is straightforward that is, but you can charge a decent price for that job, in some areas even upwards of $140 per outlet, and other areas may be even higher. Another great example is ceiling fans. The first few may take you a little while, especially if they are fancy, but after a while, if you are hustling, you should be able to replace a typical ceiling fan in about 30 minutes, and the going rate for ceiling fan replacement, at least in my area, is $150 for labor. This obviously changes from area to area, so you have to do your own research.

**Hugo Hernandez from California asks:**
*If I get a call to change a shower head only, nothing more, can I charge my minimum service fee even if it only takes me like ten minutes?*

Fantastic question, Hugo. All you can do when it comes to a minimum charge is inform the client and then let them make the decision on whether they want to hire you or not. I have told many people about our minimum, and some people get shocked and tell us we are too much. I have even had people hang up on me. At the end of the day, that is okay; they are not our ideal clients. On the other hand, I have had people tell me, "We do not have any other work that needs to be done, but we are fine paying you your minimum." These are the clients you want. I have had people who have paid me our minimum for just a ten-minute job. It all depends on the client. The best thing you can do is ask them and inform them of your rates and then let them make the final decision.

So, to answer your question more directly, if the client is fine with paying you your minimum for a ten-minute job, then that's great. If they are not fine with it, they will let you know. I would recommend that you always underpromise and overdeliver, so while you are at that ten-minute job with the awesome client, make sure their experience with you far exceeds their expectations. Take the extra time to vacuum some areas where you didn't work, play with their dog a little bit, and spend some time getting to know the client.

**Jason Michelsen from Michigan asks:**
*How do you calculate overhead, and how do you pass that on to the customer? Also, how often should you reevaluate it?*

Great question, Jason. I think for simplicity in understanding, let me define *overhead*. Overhead refers to the ongoing business expenses not directly attributed to creating a product or service. It is important for budgeting purposes but also for determining how much a company must charge for its products or services to make a profit. So basically, our business overhead is our business expenses that we figured out earlier in this book, and the way this is passed on to the customer is simply by adding that cost into our price for handyman work. If you follow the above steps and the techniques in this book to properly set your pricing, you will successfully pass that overhead on to the client and charge appropriately, so you can be confident your business will make a profit.

To answer your second question, you will need to reevaluate this pricing often, especially when you first start out and less often as your business gets more established. For the most part, I would say that this calculation needs to be revisited every time a major financial change happens in your business. This would include if you took on a new debt, increased salaries, hired new employees, etc.

**Christopher Riley Tiger Grubb from England asks:**

*Should I give discounts? For example senior citizen discounts?*

This is an excellent question and something that actually comes up a lot. If you have done even a few handyman jobs, I bet you have been asked at least once if you offer senior or military discounts. There really is no right or wrong way to go about this; it's up to your particular business if you want to offer a discount or not. We personally just recently started offering a 5 percent military discount, because I think it is a very important thing to support our brave citizens who put their lives on the line for our freedom. At the end of the day, 5 percent really doesn't come out to a whole lot, so it doesn't really affect the bottom line. We never had any discounts until recently, when one of our amazing technicians, Frank, who is a navy veteran, recommended that it would be a good sign of our appreciation and commitment to our community. Frank is a rockstar with excellent ideas, so we instantly incorporated this discount.

**Marlin Landers from California asks:**

*Does one price fit in all scenarios?*

Marlin is one of our consultant clients in our Business Builders private group, where we focus on growing our handyman businesses with employees, so he already knew the answer to his question but thought it would be a great question to add to this book, and I totally agree.

I will start my answer by quoting what he wrote regarding this answer: *"Something I had to learn was there is price, then there are other things that can make the price go up from there, like I quoted someone my standard price to swap a toilet, then when I got there, the bathroom had carpet, and the price went up from there."*

Amazing insights, Marlin. There is no such thing as one price fits all, and if someone tells you that, they are lying to you. Even if you do your due diligence and create a price list that attempts to cover all the unforeseen issues, there are still going to be unforeseen issues that come up, and you will need to be willing and able to pivot on your pricing so that you can continue to grow. Pricing, like I talked about earlier, is different for everyone and really is different for every occasion. When pricing something, you have to take into account the environment and state it is in. For instance, if you go in and price out a ceiling fan replacement, you must slow down and survey the area. Is there a bed in the way that may need to be moved? Is the ceiling fan hardwired, or is it on a switch? What if the junction box is not ceiling-fan rated? What does the drywall look like around the ceiling fan? Is the drywall going to crumble away if I disturb it? How old is the house, and what type of wiring does it most likely have?

These may seem like insignificant things to think about, but I bring them up because I have experienced them all, and they do happen. So, all in all, pricing is never one price fits all. Thanks for that question, Marlin.

**Kris Evans from Maine asks:**

*What do you do when you get stiffed?*

Great question, Kris. This is probably a topic for another book, but let's dive into it briefly. Just to be clear, what I mean by "stiffed" is a client doesn't pay you. Well, if the client decides they don't want to pay you, plainly that's messed up, because you ultimately (hopefully) had a contract, and they decided not to hold up their end of the deal. Now, we have never been stiffed, but we have had people withhold payment until we came back and performed an item a certain way. From my experience, most people are usually pretty sensible and decent. Again, I said most, not all, but that's for another time. So, if most people are sensible and decent, there has to be a reason that they felt the need to stiff you and not pay you, and my bet is that you, as the handyman, probably didn't do something entirely to their liking, and that is okay. You just need to recognize that we all make mistakes sometimes and go back and fix what needs to be done, get paid, and move on.

Now, if a client straight up won't pay you and doesn't give you any reason and won't talk to you, it may be time to get the law involved in one way or another, but I am not the consultant for that. All I know is you need to check your state laws because in some states (California for one), if a client doesn't want to pay you, as an unlicensed contractor (a handyman), legally they do not have to, and you cannot do anything about it. I know, crazy, but that's the law. So, check your state law.

**Marlin Landers from California asks:**

*How do I target the customers that will pay my prices vs. the customers that doesn't want to pay my prices?*

Attracting the right clients is another one of my huge passions, and it really has to do with marketing more than pricing. I would recommend for you to read one of our other books, *The Handyman Marketing Handbook*. In that book, we go in depth on how to attract what I call your ideal client. This client will be more focused on you and your skills than what you charge. So, simply put, it is in how you portray and market yourself that will attract the clients you want, but there are many more techniques in our other book.

Also, one huge way that you can attract and keep clients who will pay your prices is by having firm prices. If you waver on your prices, you are going to attract clients who tend to take advantage of your kind heart and walk all over you and your prices. It's the Law of Attraction. People tend to attract people who are similar to them—but it also suggests that people's thoughts tend to attract similar results. Negative thinking attracts negative experiences, while positive thinking produces desirable experiences. Stand behind your pricing and your business, and people will see that and respect that and stand behind them as well.

**Dave French from Texas asks:**

*I don't flat rate anything and charge by the hour for all services. Customers are resistant to hourly pricing, even though often it is less than what a flat rate would be. Hourly rates for everything are transparent. Is there a technique I can use that will get the customer to accept my terms?*

Great question, Dave. This is one reason why I recommend charging by the hour. Clients are usually more comfortable paying by the job than by the hour. This really has to do with mindset. People who work a day job for X amount of dollars per hour might see your business hourly rate, which is higher than what they get paid, and think it is ridiculous, even though that price you are charging is not what we take home. A lot of it goes to cover business overhead. Since we know that some clients think this way, it is easier on them to give them a per-job price than an hourly price. So, I would suggest for you to start estimating jobs by the job, rather than by the hour. Just try it out for two weeks, and then compare your sales to when you bid hourly. I would almost bet that your sales will be higher. It is interesting. A client often feels better if you tell them that it will be $100 to swap a toilet than if you tell them you're charging $100 an hour.

**Alfred Nwachukwu Udah from North Carolina asks:**

*How do I tell my current customers that my hourly rate has increased? I am getting busy, so my time is worth more than when I was starting out last year (e.g., from $20/hour to $50/hour).*

Great question, Alfred. As you go, your prices will change as circumstances change in your business, the economy changes, etc. So, having to adjust your hourly rate is something we will all need to deal with, and we all will most likely have a client who you used to work for at a certain price, and you now have to inform them of your new prices.

The best way to do this is really the whole premise of this book: be honest. This whole book is written so that you can actually know your hourly rate and need and stand firm in that because you have actual calculations to back up what you are charging. The best way to inform clients is to be honest with them by telling them exactly why your prices have gone up. Maybe you have increased overhead, or gas prices have gone up, etc.

Most of the time, you do not need to go into specifics, the conversation will go like this. "Our rates have changed a bit from the last time we worked together." The client will either say "Okay, send me an estimate," or they will say, "Okay, I will find someone else." Either way it is okay; losing one client is not the end of the world. One topic we talk about a lot in the *Handyman Marketing Handbook* is ideal clients, and an ideal client focuses more on working with you because they like you and your work rather than your prices. So, a client who focuses solely on prices may not be your ideal client.

**Brad Repka from Texas asks:**

*Will you drop your prices if a client thinks you're too high?*

I love this question. This basically has the same answer as another question but in a slightly different way. The short answer is no, I do not lower my prices. The long answer is, we strive very hard to keep our prices competitive and spend a lot of time figuring out our appropriate prices so we can help out our ideal client. So my prices are my prices because at the end of the day, my prices are what is needed to sustain and grow my business. Simply put, if my prices are too high for a client, that is okay. That client and I are just not meant to work with each other. They are not my ideal client, and I am not their ideal handyman. Now, on the other hand, if you cannot get any work at all because you refuse to drop your prices, and you are just twiddling your thumbs, waiting for a millionaire to move into your town, your prices are probably too high for your area, and you need to readjust.

**Jason Bergfeld from Washington writes:**
*Will I ever charge enough money for my service if I fear poverty?*
*(Mindset question)*
*"Faith is the starting point to all accumulation of wealth." -Napoleon Hill*
*So have faith in what you're selling ... and understand, you're doing something that 90 percent of people are too afraid to do.*
*Also*

*"The reason you're not getting $5 for your chicken eggs is because you're not asking."*

*"People won't pay that much."*

*Have you even tried asking?*

*Not much of a question, but our self-confidence takes a huge role in our pricing.*

*I went from charging $65 an hour to now bidding jobs to earn $111 to $150 an hour.*

*Basically, I had no idea it cost so much to run a business. I wanted (knew) I had to charge more, but I was scared people would not pay.*

*It took about a year, then (just recently) I got over my poverty mindset.*

*So, I started sending bids with my new (too expensive) pricing.*

*"I GOT EVEN BUSIER." Wow, how does that work?*

Amazing words of wisdom, Jason. You have to know that you are valuable and people desire the skills you have. Stand behind your business and believe that you can do this.

# Conclusion

No one knows the pricing of your handyman business better than you. You are the one who will need to perform all these calculations and make the final decisions on what your pricing needs to be. Also remember that things can be tweaked and changed from time to time. Nothing is 100 percent set in stone, so don't be afraid to pivot a little as needed. I recommend keeping this book in your glove box or desk drawer to pull out and refer to from time to time as your business grows. Remember that there is no right or wrong way to do things; you have to find what works best for your business, and what works for you may not be what works for someone else.

In conclusion, this book is composed of tips that have helped people make millions of dollars in their handyman business all around the world, and my hope is that it does the same for you. It is my honor to get to share this information with you, and I am really excited to hear how you put this into practice. Leave us a message to let us know how this book has influenced your business at handymanjourney@gmail.com.

## Your Next-Step Resources:

- If you are looking for more in-depth applied information on this pricing strategy, I would recommend you sign up for the Handyman Pricing Micro Course through www.HandymanJourney.thinkific.com. We have had dozens of handymen go through this class, and their businesses have absolutely exploded by applying this content. You can also see some testimonials at www.handymanjourney.com.

- Visit www.handymanjourney.com, where there are countless resources from e-books to full courses on many topics to take your handyman business to the next level.

- Follow The Handyman Journey on YouTube, Instagram, and Facebook to follow along on our Handyman Journey.

YouTube:

https://www.youtube.com/channel/UCHO4Ph5ithDRTski0RA0wlw

Facebook:

https://www.facebook.com/HandymanJourney/

Instagram:

https://www.instagram.com/the_handyman_journey/

- Join the conversation about others' handyman journey on The Handyman Journey mastermind group on Facebook at https://www.facebook.com/groups/955093931316242/

- Check out The Handyman Success Podcast anywhere you listen to podcasts!

Made in the USA
Las Vegas, NV
29 December 2024

15560716R00056